Joel A. Williams

TIPS IN BUILDING WEALTH AND GAINING FINANCIAL INDEPENDENCE

Embarking on Wealth building Odyssey!

Joel A. Williams

TABLE OF CONTENTS

INTRODUCTION

In the immense scene of individual budget, the quest for abundance is an excursion set apart by unmistakable stages, each requiring vital route and a sharp comprehension of monetary standards. Welcome to "Tips in Building of Wealth And Gaining Financial Independence" an exhaustive aide intended to enlighten the way toward monetary achievement. In the pages that follow, we set out on an extraordinary investigation, diving into key procedures, bits of knowledge, and rules that will enable you on your mission for enduring success.

Setting out on the Establishing a strong financial foundation Odyssey

The excursion to monetary achievement is similar to leaving on an odyssey, where each stage unfurls another section in the tale of your monetary prosperity. From establishing the groundwork to receiving the benefits, these stages are not simply steps yet achievements, each requesting consideration, responsibility, and an essential outlook.

Disentangling the Privileged insights of Monetary Success

At the core of this guide lies the obligation to reveal the privileged insights of monetary achievement. We explore past customary way of thinking, offering a nuanced comprehension of growing a substantial financial foundation that stretches out past the simple collection of money related resources. Through the investigation of each stage, we uncover the unpredictable trap of choices, propensities, and mentalities that add to a powerful and getting through monetary establishment.

Creating Your Prosperous Future

"Tips in Building Wealth and Gaining Financial Independence" is more than a guide; it's a toolbox for making your prosperous future. Whether you're simply starting your growing long term financial stability excursion or trying to refine your monetary technique, this guide gives significant bits of knowledge and functional exhortation to enable your choices. From planning essentials to cutting edge venture systems, we cover the range, guaranteeing that each peruser finds significant direction custom fitted to their novel monetary objectives.

Joining a Local area of Wealth Builders

As you submerge yourself in the pages ahead, recollect that you are in good company on this excursion. The quest for abundance is a common undertaking, and this guide welcomes you to join a local area of abundance developers. Through shared encounters, contextual investigations, and reasonable activities, you'll acquire a feeling of kinship and backing that improves your capacity to explore the difficulties and wins inborn chasing monetary success.

Embrace the Transformation

Let the pages of "Tips in Building Wealth and Gaining Financial Independence" be your buddy on this groundbreaking excursion. Embrace the change that accompanies informed navigation, restrained propensities, and a comprehensive way to deal with wealth. The insight inside these sections isn't just about collecting riches; about developing an outlook cultivates persevering through monetary achievement.

May this guide be a reference point of information, directing you through the phases of growing long term financial stability with clearness, reason, and certainty? Your monetary odyssey begins now.

CHAPTER 1: CONCEPT OF WEALTH AND FINANCIAL INDEPENDENCE

WEALTH: An Extensive Introduction

At the center of our excursion through the Phases of Creating Financial wellbeing lies the principal idea of wealth. Characterizing wealth goes past a basic identification of money related resources; it typifies a far reaching range of assets that add to an existence of overflow and satisfaction. In its substance, wealth is the collection of important resources, both unmistakable and immaterial, that upgrade one's prosperity and give an establishment to future open doors.

Aspects of Wealth

Wealth, in its diverse nature, stretches out across different aspects. Monetary resources, Intellectual Capital, social associations, wellbeing, time, and reason add to the extravagance of this idea. By recognizing these different aspects, we set up for an all-encompassing investigation of abundance that rises above customary monetary measurements.

Monetary Resources: The Conventional Pillars

Monetary resources, involving reserve funds, ventures, and property, address the customary mainstays of wealth. These resources offer an unmistakable starting point for monetary security and solidness. Understanding the job of monetary resources gives an essential point of view on the most proficient method to explore the beginning phases of establishing a strong financial foundation.

Intellectual Capital: knowledge as Currency

Intellectual Capital arises as a strong power in the abundance condition. Instruction, abilities, and information structure a cash that rises above financial worth, empowering people to pursue informed choices and immediately jump all over chances. We dive into the idea of scholarly riches, underlining its job as a dynamic and valuing resource.

Social Capital: The Power of Relationships

Wealth stretches out past individual undertakings and embraces the force of connections. Social capital, got from significant associations and organizations, improves open doors for cooperation, mentorship, and shared assets. Investigating the meaning of social associations adds a social aspect to the establishing a strong financial foundation venture.

Wellbeing and Prosperity: Foundation of Prosperity

Genuine wealth envelops more than material belongings; it incorporates the underpinning of wellbeing and prosperity. Physical and mental prosperity are necessary parts that support a prosperous life. This part examines the cooperative connection among wellbeing and riches, underlining the significance of a reasonable and supportable way to deal with both.

Time: A Valuable Asset

Time is a currency with a special incentive. This part dives into the idea of time wealth, featuring the essential administration of time as a critical consider building enduring flourishing. Understanding how to use time really adds to long haul monetary achievement.

Purpose and Passion: Satisfaction in Wealth

Wealth finds its definitive satisfaction when lined up with purpose and enthusiasm. This part welcomes perusers to investigate the crossing point of individual qualities and monetary objectives. By injecting establishing long term financial stability with reason, people make a story that goes past money related gains, adding to an existence of importance and importance.

In unwinding the layers of wealth, we establish the groundwork for a far reaching understanding that stretches out past customary monetary ideal models. Remember that wealth is a dynamic and developing idea, molded by a blend of unmistakable and elusive resources that all in all characterize a daily routine very much experienced.

Monetary Independence: Securing Your Monetary Future

Understanding Monetary Independence

Monetary freedom remains as a foundation in the excursion through the "Phases of Creating Financial stability." At its center, monetary autonomy is the state where an individual has adequate monetary assets to support their ideal way of life without being dependent on outside types of revenue. This part dives into the complexities of monetary autonomy, investigating not exclusively its definition yet in addition the significant effect it can have on one's life.

Breaking Free from Monetary Constraints

The charm of monetary autonomy lies in the opportunity it manages. This segment investigates breaking liberated from the shackles of monetary requirements, freeing people from the check to-check cycle. Accomplishing monetary freedom enables people to go with life decisions in view of individual objectives as opposed to monetary commitments.

Creating financial wellbeing as a Way to Monetary Independence

We take apart the advantageous connection between creating financial stability and achieving monetary freedom. The essential gathering of resources, combined with careful monetary propensities, arises as the guide toward monetary independence. Understanding the connection between growing a strong financial foundation and monetary freedom is crucial in exploring the stages ahead.

Backup stash and Monetary Security

Vital to monetary autonomy is the foundation of a backup stash. This wellbeing net gives a cushion against unanticipated conditions, offering genuine serenity and strength even with startling costs. We examine the significance of crisis assets as a central component chasing monetary freedom.

Recurring, automated revenue: The Impetus for Freedom

Recurring, automated revenue fills in as an impetus for monetary freedom, permitting people to produce income with negligible continuous exertion. This part investigates different roads for making automated sources of income, from speculations to undertakings, featuring their job in facilitating the excursion to monetary independence.

The purpose of Budgeting and Monetary Discipline

Budgeting arises as an urgent device in the mission for monetary freedom. This part accentuates the meaning of trained monetary propensities, judicious spending, and key reserve funds. By becoming amazing at planning, people lay the basis for maintainable monetary freedom.

Exploring Debt and Credit

Debt can be a huge obstruction on the way to monetary freedom. This part tends to procedures for overseeing and paying off past commitments, engaging people to defeat monetary difficulties and speed up their advancement toward independence. Understanding the nuanced connection among obligation and independence from the rat race is critical in accomplishing enduring outcomes.

The Psychological effect of Monetary Independence

Beyond the monetary angles, accomplishing autonomy makes significant psychological impacts. We investigate the attitude shifts and newly discovered certainty that go with monetary freedom. This part digs into the inward feeling of harmony, diminished pressure, and expanded feeling of control that accompany breaking liberated from monetary reliance.

Understanding Your Vision of Monetary Independence

As we close this section, it is fundamental to perceive that monetary freedom is a customized venture. Perusers are urged to imagine their exceptional rendition of monetary independence, adjusting their objectives to a feeling of direction. This part lays the basis for the resulting stages, where the standards of monetary autonomy will keep on molding the direction of growing a substantial financial foundation.

The Significance of Monetary Autonomy: Engaging Your Future

Monetary freedom isn't only a monetary achievement; it's a groundbreaking state with broad ramifications for each part of life. In this segment, we dig into the significant significance of accomplishing monetary freedom and how it turns into an impetus for strengthening and satisfaction.

1. Security in Dubious Times

Monetary freedom fills in as a vigorous safeguard notwithstanding financial vulnerabilities. In the midst of unanticipated difficulties like employment cutback, monetary slumps, or unforeseen costs, the monetarily autonomous individual is better prepared to face the hardship. This layer of monetary security gives inner harmony and a feeling of command over one's predetermination.

2. Opportunity to Seek after Passion

Accomplishing monetary autonomy opens the ways to seeking after meaningful ventures and individual interests. Whether it's beginning a business, voyaging, or taking part in magnanimity, the independence from monetary limitations permits people to adjust their activities to their interests. This freshly discovered freedom adds to a really satisfying and reason driven life.

3. Flexibility in Life Choices

Monetary autonomy engages people to settle on important decisions in light of individual qualities as opposed to monetary limitations. Whether it's picking a profession for enthusiasm instead of need or choosing when and how to resign, the capacity to settle on decisions without being limited by monetary commitments upgrades the personal satisfaction and adds to in general prosperity.

4. Stress Decrease and Improved Mental Health

Breaking free from the pattern of monetary pressure is one of the main advantages of monetary freedom. The decrease of monetary uneasiness adds to worked on psychological wellness, encouraging a positive outlook and upgrading generally speaking life fulfillment. The genuine serenity that goes with monetary autonomy is a significant resource in the present quick moving and flighty world.

5. Legacy Building and Generational Impact

Monetary freedom gives the chance to fabricate a lasting legacy. Whether it includes leaving a legacy for people in the future, supporting worthy missions, or having a constructive outcome on the local area, the monetarily free individual can make a heritage that reaches out past their lifetime. This feeling of heritage building adds a significant aspect to the significance of monetary freedom.

6. Strengthening in Choice Making

Monetary autonomy engages people to settle on choices in view of what lines up with their qualities and long haul objectives as opposed to being influenced by quick monetary necessities. This strengthening in direction reaches out to different parts of life, from profession decisions to significant life changes, encouraging a feeling of control and independence.

7. Exiting the workforce and Broadened Leisure

For some, the fantasy of exiting the workforce turns into a reality with monetary freedom. The capacity to resign early and appreciate broadened relaxation time is a substantial advantage. This segment investigates the methodologies and contemplations for those seeking to resign early, stressing the significance of monetary freedom in acknowledging such yearnings.

8. Autonomy in Choice Making

Monetary freedom gives an exceptional type of freedom in direction. People are freed from pursuing decisions exclusively founded on monetary requirements, permitting them to adjust their choices to their qualities, yearnings, and long haul vision. This opportunity stretches out to vocation choices, pioneering pursuits, and way of life decisions, cultivating a feeling of independence and self-assurance.

9. Enterprising Endeavors and Risk Taking

For yearning business visionaries, monetary freedom fills in as a wellbeing net that empowers risk-taking. The capacity to seek after pioneering adventures or put resources into creative thoughts turns out to be more attainable when the apprehension about monetary unsteadiness is relieved. This segment investigates how monetary freedom establishes a climate helpful for embracing carefully thought out plans of action and chasing after enterprising aspirations.

10. Further developed Connections and quality of Life

Monetary freedom decidedly impacts individual connections and by and large personal satisfaction. Decreased monetary pressure frequently prompts better connections, as people can zero in on shared objectives and encounters as opposed to monetary battles. Besides, a better personal satisfaction reaches out past material solaces, enveloping encounters, relaxation, and a more adjusted way of life.

11. Charitable Contribution and Social Impact

Monetary freedom enhances a singular's ability to add to worthy missions and have a positive social effect. Whether through generosity, chipping in, or supporting local area drives, monetarily free people can assume a more dynamic part in adding to the prosperity of society. This segment investigates the job of monetary freedom in encouraging a feeling of social obligation.

12. Redefining the Meaning of Work

Monetary autonomy permits people to reclassify the importance of work in their lives. Rather than survey work exclusively for the purpose of monetary food, people can investigate profession ways that line up with their interests and values. This change in context adds to a seriously satisfying and reason driven way to deal with proficient life.

13. Flexibility notwithstanding Monetary Challenges

In the midst of monetary difficulties, people with monetary autonomy are better situated to explore vulnerabilities. This segment dives into the strength that monetary freedom gives, empowering people to adjust to financial vacillations, work market changes, and unexpected conditions no sweat.

14. Education and Individual Development

Monetary autonomy opens roads for ceaseless schooling and self-improvement. Whether seeking after postgraduate educations, going to studios, or participating in deep rooted learning, monetarily free people have the adaptability to put resources into their scholarly capital. This obligation to progressing instruction improves their abilities and information, adding to self-awareness and expert headway.

Understanding these extra elements of the significance of monetary freedom gives a more complete perspective on its groundbreaking effect. As we progress through the phases of growing a strong financial foundation, these experiences will keep on illuminating our way to deal with making enduring monetary progress.

In perceiving the diverse significance of monetary freedom, people gain a more profound comprehension of its extraordinary power. As we progress through the phases of creating financial momentum, the standards of monetary freedom will proceed to guide and shape our way to deal with monetary achievement.

CHAPTER 2: CONCEPT OF FINANCIAL EDUCATION

Monetary Education: Empowering Mind for Wealth Mastery

The Essence of Monetary Education

As we explore through the phases of creating financial momentum, the role of monetary instruction arises as a directing power. Monetary training isn't just about numbers and bookkeeping sheets; the key opens the ways to informed direction, key preparation, and long haul monetary achievement. In this section, we dive into the pith of monetary schooling and its extraordinary effect on people looking to excel at abundance collection.

1. Building an Underpinning of Monetary Literacy

Monetary instruction starts with the advancement of monetary education. This segment investigates the key ideas, wording, and rules that lay the basis for grasping the complexities of individual budget. Building a strong underpinning of monetary education furnishes people with the information important to explore the intricacies of the monetary world.

2. The Force of Informed Choice Making

At the core of monetary education lies the force of informed independent direction. By equipping people with the information to survey gambles, assess open doors, and comprehend the ramifications of monetary decisions, this section shows how monetary education turns into an essential device in molding a way to riches. Through certifiable models and contextual investigations, we represent the effect of informed dynamic on monetary results.

3. Objective Setting and Monetary Planning

Monetary education enables people to put forth clear monetary objectives and foster extensive designs to accomplish them. This segment investigates the course of objective setting, underlining the significance of adjusting monetary goals to individual qualities. From the perspective of monetary schooling, perusers gain bits of knowledge into making vital monetary plans that prepare for long haul achievement.

4. Exploring the Venture Landscape

Understanding the speculation scene is an urgent part of monetary schooling. This part digs into the different venture vehicles, risk the board methodologies, and the standards of portfolio broadening. By demystifying the universe of speculations, monetary instruction empowers people to go with sound venture choices that add to abundance amassing.

5. Debt management and Credit Literacy

Monetary education stretches out to the domain of obligation the board and credit proficiency. This part investigates systems for dependable getting, compelling obligation reimbursement, and building a positive record of loan repayment. By furnishing people with the information to explore obligation carefully, monetary schooling turns into a device for keeping up with monetary wellbeing and steadiness.

6. Tax Planning and Optimization

Exploring the complexities of Tax Planning is a fundamental part of monetary education. This part examines the standards of tax streamlining, investigating techniques for limiting assessment liabilities and amplifying returns. Through pragmatic experiences and models, perusers gain a comprehension of how vital expense arranging adds to in general monetary prosperity.

7. Adjusting to Economic Changes

Monetary education cultivates flexibility notwithstanding financial changes. Whether exploring monetary slumps, market variances, or changes in monetary guidelines, people with strong monetary schooling are more ready to adjust and pursue informed choices. This segment features the versatility that accompanies monetary instruction.

8. Inheritance Arranging and Wealth Preservation

As people progress in their establishing financial stability venture, monetary schooling becomes instrumental in heritage arranging and abundance safeguarding. This part investigates systems for bequest arranging, abundance move, and the conservation of resources for people in the future. Through a complete comprehension of these standards, people can leave an enduring heritage that reaches out past their lifetime.

9. Embracing Persistent Learning

Monetary education is a deep rooted venture. This part stresses the significance of embracing nonstop learning and keeping up to date with advancing monetary scenes. By developing a mentality of continuous schooling, people position themselves for supported monetary achievement and versatility in a unique financial climate.

10. Cultivating Monetary Confidence

At last, monetary training adds to encouraging monetary certainty. This part investigates how a very much educated individual is more prepared to confront monetary difficulties, settle on essential choices, and explore the intricacies of growing a substantial financial foundation with certainty. Monetary instruction turns into the impetus for changing trepidation into strengthening.

As we progress through the phases of creating financial momentum, the standards of monetary instruction will keep on directing our excursion. By embracing the substance of monetary instruction, people leave on a groundbreaking way towards excelling at abundance gathering and getting a prosperous future.

Significance of Monetary Education: Engaging Lives for Prosperity

Monetary Education remains as a guide of strengthening, enlightening the way to monetary prosperity and success. In this sweeping investigation, we dive into the significant meaning of monetary schooling, disentangling its effect on people, families, and networks. As we progress through the phases of creating financial wellbeing, understanding the extensive ramifications of monetary instruction becomes central.

The Underpinning of Informed Decision Making

Monetary instruction frames the bedrock of informed direction. As people secure information about planning, ventures, and obligation the executives, they gain the apparatuses to settle on sound monetary decisions. This basic comprehension enables them to explore the intricacies of the monetary scene with certainty, making way for a long period of judicious independent direction.

Breaking the Pattern of Monetary Stress

One of the main commitments of monetary training is its capacity to break the pattern of monetary pressure. By conferring fundamental abilities for planning, reserve funds, and obligation the executives, monetary schooling outfits people with the means to proactively address their monetary difficulties. This recently discovered command over individual budgets lessens pressure, encouraging mental prosperity and versatility despite monetary vulnerabilities.

Cultivating Financial Incorporation and Equity

Monetary education assumes a vital part in cultivating financial consideration and value. This segment investigates how admittance to monetary information enables people from assorted foundations to take part more really in the economy. By crossing over the data hole, monetary schooling turns into an impetus for diminishing incongruities and advancing financial value inside networks.

Reinforcing Family Monetary Stability

At the family level, monetary instruction adds to reinforced monetary dependability. Through experiences into powerful planning, saving techniques, and judicious monetary preparation, families can climate financial difficulties and fabricate an establishment for long haul security. This segment frames how monetary instruction changes families into tough monetary units.

Empowering Entrepreneurs and Little Businesses

For business visionaries and entrepreneurs, monetary instruction turns into an essential partner. This fragment investigates how a strong comprehension of monetary standards improves business sharpness, empowering business people to settle on informed choices, oversee income successfully, and explore the intricacies of business with certainty.

Exploring the Venture Landscape

Understanding the venture scene is a critical part of monetary instruction. This page digs into how monetary schooling engages people to pursue informed speculation choices, encouraging abundance collection and monetary development. From investigating different resource classes to getting a handle on risk the board techniques, monetary training turns into a directing power in the excursion towards monetary freedom.

Improving Retirement Planning

As people plan for their retirement, monetary instruction turns into a significant resource. This part investigates how information about retirement reserve funds, speculation techniques, and benefits plans enables people to make exhaustive retirement plans. Monetary instruction turns into the compass directing people towards a protected and satisfying retirement.

Advancing Monetary Obligation across Generations

The meaning of monetary schooling stretches out past individual lives; it shapes the monetary obligation of people in the future. This page features how imparting monetary proficiency in more youthful ages adds to a tradition of informed direction, making a gradually expanding influence of monetary prosperity that rises above time.

Adjusting to Financial Changes

In a consistently developing monetary scene, the flexibility encouraged by monetary schooling becomes vital. This part investigates how people furnished with monetary information are more ready to explore financial changes, market vacillations, and worldwide vulnerabilities, guaranteeing strength and vital independent direction.

Adding to Social and Community Well-being

The last page investigates the cultural effect of monetary instruction. By engaging people with the apparatuses to accomplish monetary steadiness, monetary training adds to generally local area prosperity. From lessening the weight on friendly administrations to advancing an all the more monetarily engaged populace, the meaning of monetary schooling stretches out a long ways past individual lives.

Taking everything into account, the meaning of monetary schooling couldn't possibly be more significant. A groundbreaking power engages people, fortifies families, and adds to the financial prosperity of networks. As we progress through the phases of creating financial stability, the getting through effect of monetary schooling will keep on molding our way to deal with thriving.

Defining Monetary Objectives and Creating a Budget: Blueprint for Monetary Success

Laying out clear monetary objectives and making a spending plan are essential strides in the excursion towards monetary achievement. In this investigation, we dive into the meaning of laying out distinct monetary targets and creating an essential spending plan that lines up with these objectives.

Laying out Monetary Objectives: A Guide to Success

Monetary objectives act as a guide, giving guidance and inspiration to your establishing financial stability venture. This segment digs into the significance of setting explicit, quantifiable, reachable, pertinent, and time-bound (Shrewd) monetary objectives. Whether it's putting something aside for a home, subsidizing schooling, or building a backup stash, articulating clear targets turns into the most important move toward monetary achievement.

1. Characterizing Present moment and Long haul Goals

Monetary objectives include both present moment and long haul yearnings. This page investigates the differentiation between these objectives, stressing the significance of offsetting prompt monetary requirements with future goals. By understanding the timetable of objectives, people can foster a dynamic and practical way to deal with establishing financial stability.

2. Focusing on and Arranging Goals

Not all monetary objectives are made equivalent. This part directs people in focusing on and sorting their objectives in view of earnestness and significance. By laying out a pecking order, people can dispense assets successfully, guaranteeing that fundamental objectives are tended to prior to seeking after more optimistic goals.

3. Adjusting Objectives to Values and Aspirations

The arrangement of monetary objectives with individual qualities and desires is foremost. This page investigates the significant effect of laying out objectives that impact one's guiding principle.

By guaranteeing that monetary targets line up with more extensive life goals, people make a more significant and reason driven growing a strong financial foundation venture.

4. Evaluating Objectives and Making Milestones

Evaluating monetary objectives and breaking them into reasonable achievements gives a substantial system to progress. This segment dives into the most common way of relegating explicit numbers to objectives and making feasible achievements. By changing dynamic yearnings into quantifiable targets, people gain clearness on their advancement and change their techniques as needs be.

Making a Spending plan: Your Monetary Compass

A spending plan isn't only a device for following costs; a unique monetary compass directs your excursion toward monetary objectives. This section investigates the meaning of making a spending plan, enumerating how this cycle enables people to oversee assets really, save in a calculated way, and remain on track to accomplish their monetary targets.

❖ Income Evaluation and Cost Analysis

Understanding your income sources and breaking down costs are basic moves toward making a financial plan. This page investigates how people can survey their month to month pay, sort sources, and lead an exhaustive examination of costs. By acquiring an unmistakable outline, people set up for informed monetary direction.

❖ Fixed versus Variable Expenses

Recognizing fixed and variable costs is vital for planning achievement. This part dives into the distinction between these two classifications and investigates procedures for dealing with each successfully. By ordering costs, people can distinguish regions for expected reserve funds and assign assets all the more decisively.

❖ Building an Emergency Fund

Planning incorporates arrangements for building and keeping a rainy day account. This page accentuates the significance of saving assets for unexpected conditions. By integrating a backup stash into the spending plan, people make a monetary wellbeing net, giving security and strength notwithstanding surprising costs.

❖ Reserve funds and Speculation Allocation

Planning works with the assignment of assets to reserve funds and speculations. This part investigates techniques for saving cash for present moment and long haul reserve funds objectives. By integrating venture commitments into the spending plan, people outfit the force of compounding and speed up progress toward monetary freedom.

❖ Debt Reimbursement Strategies

Tending to debt is a basic part of planning. This page digs into successful techniques for obligation reimbursement, stressing the significance of dispensing a piece of the spending plan to decrease and kill exceptional obligations. By integrating obligation reimbursement into the spending plan, people move toward independence from the rat race.

❖ Standard Budget Surveys and Adjustments

A financial plan is a powerful instrument that requires normal surveys and changes. This part investigates the significance of occasionally assessing the spending plan, evaluating progress toward monetary objectives, and making important changes. By taking on an adaptable methodology, people can guarantee that their spending plan stays lined up with developing monetary conditions.

❖ Involving Innovation and Apparatuses for Budgeting

Technology tools assume an urgent part in present day planning. This page investigates different planning applications, programming, and devices that improve on the planning system. By tackling the capacities of innovation, people get to continuous bits of knowledge, robotized following, and smoothed out spending plan the executives.

❖ Developing a Planning Mindset

Past the numbers, developing a planning mentality is fundamental for long haul achievement. This part dives into the mental parts of planning, tending to normal difficulties and offering techniques for fostering a positive and feasible way to deal with overseeing funds.

Putting forth monetary objectives and making a financial plan are indispensable parts of a vital and reason driven growing a substantial financial foundation venture. As people leave on this way, the standards investigated in this part will act as a compass, directing them toward monetary achievement and satisfaction.

CHAPTER 3: INCOME GENERATION

Concept of Income: Beyond Dollars and Cents

The idea of income isn't bound to the dollars and pennies on a check; it is a diverse part of our monetary lives. In this investigation, we dig into the assorted elements of pay, investigating its different sources, suggestions, and the crucial job it plays in forming our monetary prosperity.

Grasping Income: Beyond Financial Value

Income is in excess of a mathematical portrayal of profit; a powerful power impacts our ways of life, potential open doors, and monetary objectives. This part investigates the more extensive comprehension of pay, incorporating compensation as well as extra sources like ventures, rental pay, and second jobs. By perceiving the different types of pay, people can use a complete way to deal with establishing long term financial stability.

1. Procured Income: The Groundwork of Monetary Stability

Procured pay, got from work and work, fills in as the primary component of monetary security. This page dives into the meaning of procured pay, underlining its part in gathering day to day expenses, subsidizing reserve funds objectives, and giving the fundamental assets to an agreeable way of life. Understanding how procured pay lines up with monetary objectives is urgent in the establishing a strong financial foundation venture.

2. Recurring, automated Income: The Motor of Monetary Independence

Recurring, automated revenue addresses profit created with insignificant dynamic contribution. This segment investigates the idea of recurring, automated revenue, emerging from speculations, investment properties, or undertakings. By developing automated sources of income, people lay the preparation for monetary autonomy, opening the possibility to support their ideal way of life without consistent dynamic work.

Venture Income: Developing Abundance Through Capital

Investment income is a critical part of the establishing financial stability condition. This page digs into the different types of speculation pay, including profits, interest, and capital increases. Understanding how to streamline venture portfolios to produce pay adds to the drawn out development of abundance and monetary security.

Side hustles and Extra Revenue Streams

The advanced scene of pay stretches out past conventional business. This segment investigates the idea of part time jobs and extra revenue sources, stressing how people can use their abilities and interests to make valuable kinds of revenue. Broadening revenue streams upgrades monetary soundness as well as opens roads for individual and expert development.

Social Capital: Utilizing Network for Opportunities

Social capital, while not money related in nature, assumes an urgent part in pay age. This page investigates how connections, organizations, and associations can add to pay amazing open doors. From work references to business joint efforts, social capital turns into an important resource that extends pay potential and opens ways to additional opportunities.

Close to home and Profound Pay: Past Monetary Metrics

Pay isn't exclusively about monetary measurements; it additionally includes close to home and profound aspects. This part digs into the idea of profound pay, got from satisfying work and positive connections. Furthermore, otherworldly pay emerges from adjusting one's qualities and reason to their expert undertakings, adding to a feeling of significance and satisfaction past monetary benefits.

Overseeing Income: Planning, Saving, and Investing

Successfully overseeing pay is a basic expertise in the establishing long term financial stability venture. This page investigates the down to earth parts of pay the board, including planning to control costs, saving to construct a monetary pad, and contributing to develop riches. By taking on sound monetary practices, people can boost the effect of their pay on generally speaking monetary prosperity.

Income and Way of life Choices

Income significantly impacts way of life decisions. This part investigates how people can adjust their pay to their ideal way of life, underscoring the significance of cognizant direction. From lodging decisions to relaxation exercises, understanding the connection among pay and way of life empowers people to go with decisions that add to both monetary soundness and individual fulfillment.

Profession Improvement and income Growth

Profession improvement is complicatedly connected to pay development. This page investigates systems for progressing in one's profession, obtaining new abilities, and haggling for higher remuneration. By effectively overseeing profession directions, people can upgrade their procuring potential and make a pathway to expanded pay after some time.

Income and Monetary Objectives Alignment

The arrangement of pay with monetary objectives is critical for a reason driven establishing long term financial stability venture. This segment investigates how people can decisively distribute their pay to help present moment and long haul monetary goals. By guaranteeing cognizance among pay and objectives, people make a guide for making monetary progress and understanding their yearnings.

All in all, the idea of pay reaches out a long ways past monetary exchanges; a powerful power shapes our lives in different ways. By exhaustively understanding the different elements of pay, people can upgrade their procuring potential, pursue informed monetary choices, and set out on an all-encompassing excursion towards flourishing.

Methodologies for increasing income: Opening Your Acquiring Potential

Expanding income is a unique interaction that includes a blend of vital preparation, expertise improvement, and utilizing potential open doors. In this investigation, we dive into an exhaustive arrangement of procedures pointed toward enabling people to support their procuring potential and accomplish monetary objectives.

1. Nonstop Skill Development

Putting resources into nonstop expertise improvement is a strong methodology for expanding pay. This segment underlines the significance of remaining important in a quickly developing position market. Whether through proper training, online courses, or studios, procuring new abilities upgrades proficient skill, making people more important resources for businesses and clients.

2. Exchange Skill for Compensation

Exchange skill assume a significant part in getting positive pay bundles. This page investigates powerful exchange procedures, from compensation dealings to contract conversations for consultants and business people. By dominating exchange methods, people can guarantee that their pay mirrors their aptitude and commitments.

3. Broadening Income Streams

Broadening income streams is a critical rule in expanding by and large procuring potential. This segment investigates how people can make various types of revenue, like part time jobs, speculations, and recurring sources of income. Expansion gives monetary solidness as well as opens up open doors for outstanding pay development.

4. Entrepreneurship and Business Ventures

Leaving on business venture or beginning an undertaking can be an extraordinary methodology for expanding pay. This page investigates the enterprising outlook, stressing the significance of recognizing market needs, fostering a field-tested strategy, and developing strength. Business venture permits people to set out their pay open doors and open limitless procuring potential.

5. Networking and Relationship Building

Building a hearty expert organization is an essential resource in pay development. This part investigates the force of systems administration, underscoring the significance of developing connections inside and past one's industry. Organizing opens ways to new open doors, joint efforts, and potential revenue streams through references and organizations.

6. Putting resources into Attractive Talents

Recognizing and putting resources into attractive gifts is a proactive way to deal with expanding pay. This page investigates how people can evaluate their special abilities and gifts, perceiving those with high market interest. By diverting endeavors into creating and showcasing these gifts, people position themselves for open doors that can essentially affect their pay.

7. Utilizing Innovation and Online Platforms

In the computerized age, utilizing innovation and online stages can expand pay roads. This part investigates how people can utilize innovation to feature their abilities, offer administrations, or sell items on the web. From outsourcing stages to online business, the computerized scene gives various chances to contact a more extensive crowd and increment pay.

8. Professional success and Promotions

Decisively progressing in one's vocation is a customary yet powerful manner to increment pay. This page investigates the means people can take to situate themselves for advancements, including exhibiting authority characteristics, taking on extra obligations, and displaying commitments to authoritative achievement. Professional success frequently prompts higher acquiring potential.

9. Making and Adapting Individual Branding

Building an individual brand and adapting it is a contemporary way to deal with pay development. This part investigates how people can lay out major areas of strength for a presence, foster an individual brand, and gain by it through roads like supported content, member showcasing, or making and selling computerized items. Adapting individual marking can turn out a reasonable and versatile revenue source.

10. Land and Automated revenue Investments

Putting resources into land and other automated revenue valuable open doors is a drawn out procedure for abundance gathering. This page investigates how people can decisively put resources into investment properties, profit paying stocks, or other pay creating resources. Recurring, automated revenue speculations can give a constant flow of pay without requiring steady dynamic inclusion.

11. Chasing after High level training and Certifications

High level training and certificates frequently lead to particular abilities that order higher pay. This segment investigates how chasing after postgraduate educations or industry-explicit certificates can improve one's expert standing and pay potential. Schooling is a speculation that can yield significant returns as expanded procuring limit.

12. Geographic Arbitrage

Geographic Arbitrage includes decisively living in areas with a lower typical cost for most everyday items while procuring pay from areas with a higher pay potential. This page investigates how people can use geographic arbitrage, whether through remote work valuable open doors, outsourcing, or laying out organizations in areas with ideal financial circumstances.

13. Making and Selling Scholarly Property

Protected innovation, including books, courses, and computerized items, can be a worthwhile revenue source. This part investigates how people can make important protected innovation and adapt it through different stages. Making and offering licensed innovation permits people to use their mastery and imagination for extra pay.

14. Looking for Proficient Progression and Designations

Looking for proficient headway through industry-explicit assignments and confirmations is an essential move for money development. This page investigates how people can distinguish pertinent expert assignments, like turning into a Certified Financial Planner (CFP) or a Project Management Professional (PMP), to improve their validity and procuring potential.

In essence, expanding income is a dynamic and diverse cycle that requires a proactive and vital methodology. By consolidating these systems, people can open their full acquiring potential, making ready for monetary achievement and satisfaction.

Concept of Multiple Income Streams: Building Monetary Resilience

The idea of numerous revenue streams is a strong procedure for accomplishing monetary versatility and opening a more differentiated way to deal with growing long term financial stability. In this investigation, we dive into the meaning of developing different revenue sources, investigating the different kinds and the extraordinary effect they can have on a person's monetary scene.

Understanding Numerous Revenue Sources: An All encompassing Way to deal with Wealth

The idea of different revenue streams includes creating income from different sources past a customary regular work. This segment investigates the central thought that depending on a solitary kind of revenue can be restricting and possibly defenseless. By expanding revenue sources, people make a hearty monetary establishment that improves security, adaptability, and the potential for long haul thriving.

1. Primary Revenue Source: The Underpinning of Monetary Stability

The essential revenue stream normally begins from conventional work or a primary wellspring of business income. This page underscores the central job of the essential revenue stream in gathering fundamental costs, supporting way of life decisions, and giving a base to establishing financial stability tries. While vital, perceiving the expected constraints of a solitary pay source makes way for investigating extra streams.

2. Secondary Revenue Sources: Extending Monetary Horizons

Optional revenue streams supplement the essential source and offer extra monetary help. This segment investigates different optional streams like side gigs, independent work, or part-time undertakings. These streams add to expanded pay as well as proposition open doors for expertise advancement, vocation investigation, and individual satisfaction.

3. Passive Revenue Sources: Procuring While You Sleep

Automated sources of income include profit with negligible dynamic association. This page investigates different types of recurring, automated revenue, including profits from speculations, rental pay, sovereignties, and subsidiary showcasing. Developing automated sources of income permits people to create financial stability while diminishing reliance on nonstop dynamic work.

4. Portfolio Income: Tackling the Force of Investments

Portfolio income is gotten from venture exercises, like capital gains and interest. This part digs into the idea of building a differentiated speculation portfolio to produce predictable returns. By decisively distributing assets to different venture roads, people can develop a solid wellspring of portfolio pay.

5. Entrepreneurial Pay: Making and Scaling Businesses

Pioneering pay emerges from beginning and scaling organizations. This page investigates the pioneering outlook, underscoring how people can distinguish business amazing open doors, make items or administrations, and create income. Enterprising undertakings add to pay enhancement as well as deal a pathway to monetary freedom.

6. Online Pay: Bridling the Computerized Economy

The advanced scene gives open doors to online revenue sources, including web based business, subsidiary showcasing, and content creation. This segment investigates how people can use online stages to produce pay, taking advantage of a worldwide crowd and differentiating income sources through the extensive reach of the web.

7. Rental Pay: Land as an Income Generator

Land speculations can yield rental pay through properties like private or business rentals. This page investigates the idea of procuring pay through land, stressing the potential for both present moment and long haul returns. Rental pay gives a substantial resource and a constant flow of income.

8. Consulting and Training: Adapting Expertise

Adapting skill through counseling or training administrations is a significant revenue source. This segment digs into how people can use their insight and abilities to offer specific administrations, charging expenses for conferences, preparing, or tutoring. Counseling and instructing turn out a customized revenue stream in view of individual mastery.

9. Affiliate Marketing: Cooperative Income Generation

Subsidiary showcasing includes procuring commissions by advancing other organizations' items or administrations. This page investigates how people can participate in associate showcasing, making extra pay by driving deals or leads for accomplice organizations. This cooperative way to deal with income age use existing organizations and online stages.

10. Royalties: Income from Scholarly Property

Sovereignties address pay acquired from the utilization of licensed innovation, like books, music, or licenses. This segment investigates how people can produce eminences by permitting or offering the privileges to their inventive or scholarly works. Sovereignties give a wellspring of continuous pay in light of the proceeded with utilization of the protected innovation.

11. Educational Projects and Courses: Sharing Information for Profit

Making and selling instructive projects or courses is a suitable revenue source, especially in the computerized period. This page investigates how people can bundle their skill into instructive substance, offering it to a more extensive crowd for a charge. Instructive projects turn out a versatile revenue source while adding to information sharing.

12. Partnerships and Joint efforts: Intensifying Pay Potential

Organizations and joint efforts can enhance pay potential by consolidating assets and contacting more extensive crowds. This part investigates how people can frame unions with different organizations, business visionaries, or powerhouses to make joint endeavors. Cooperative endeavors can prompt shared income streams and extended open doors.

13. Government and Confidential Awards: Subsidizing for Projects

Getting awards, whether from government offices or confidential associations, can give financing to explicit activities. This page investigates how people and organizations can apply for awards to help drives in regions like examination, advancement, or local area improvement. Awards offer a modern yet effective type of revenue.

14. Dividend Income: Gets back from Offer Ownership

Profit pay is procured through responsibility for paying stocks. This segment digs into how people can fabricate an arrangement of profit stocks to get ordinary profit installments. Profit pay gives a solid and possibly developing stream of profits from value speculations.

15. Selling Items: Online business and Retail Ventures

Selling items, whether physical or computerized, through online business stages or retail adventures, is a substantial revenue source. This page investigates how people can create and advertise items to produce income. Selling items takes into consideration direct pay age through deals exchanges.

16. Event Facilitating and Speaking Commitment: Adapting Presence

Event facilitating and talking commitment offer chances to adapt presence and ability. This part investigates how people can get talking commitment at gatherings, studios, or occasions, procuring expenses for sharing experiences and information. Facilitating occasions likewise gives a stage to extra pay through sponsorships and ticket deals.

17. Membership and Membership Models: Repeating Revenue

Executing enrollment or membership models can make repeating revenue sources. This page investigates how people can offer selective substance, administrations, or items to supporters who pay customary expenses. Enrollment and membership models give an anticipated and progressing wellspring of income.

18. Mentorship and Instructing Projects: Directing for Profit

Laying out mentorship or instructing programs is a customized method for creating pay. This segment investigates how people can offer organized mentorship or training administrations, charging expenses for customized direction and backing. Mentorship and instructing programs influence individual skill to make an incentive for clients.

19. Crowdfunding: People group Upheld Funding

Crowdfunding includes raising assets from a local area of allies for explicit ventures or drives. This page investigates how people can utilize crowdfunding stages to earn monetary help for inventive undertakings, pioneering adventures, or altruistic tasks. Crowdfunding takes advantage of aggregate commitments for money age.

20. Licensing and Diversifying: Extending Income Reach

Permitting licensed innovation or diversifying business ideas permits people to extend pay reach. This segment dives into how people can permit their manifestations or establishment their effective plans of action, procuring pay through sovereignties or establishment charges. Authorizing and diversifying offer roads for adaptable pay development.

Advantages of Different Revenue Sources: Improving Monetary Stability

The advantages of developing different revenue streams stretch out past the immediate effect on profit. This page investigates how broadening pay sources improves monetary soundness by giving versatility against financial vulnerabilities, decreasing reliance on a solitary source, and making a more versatile monetary profile.

1. Risk Moderation and Resilience

Broadening income streams mitigates the effect of financial slumps or unanticipated conditions influencing a particular source. This part investigates how having numerous kinds of revenue diminishes weakness to startling difficulties, encouraging monetary strength and flexibility.

2. Income Dependability and Predictability

The blend of different revenue streams adds to a steadier and unsurprising monetary circumstance. This page digs into how various streams might have different execution designs, making a reasonable in general pay profile. Soundness and consistency improve monetary preparation and objective accomplishment.

3. Opportunities for Development and Abundance Accumulation

Various revenue streams give open doors to ceaseless development and abundance aggregation. This segment investigates how every revenue source, whether dynamic or uninvolved, adds to the by and large monetary picture. The aggregate impact can prompt sped up growing long term financial stability and expanded monetary security.

4. Flexibility and Way of life Choices

Different revenue streams offer adaptability in way of life decisions. This page investigates how people with different pay sources have the adaptability to make profession changes, seek after private interests, or adjust to evolving conditions. Adaptability turns into a critical advantage of pay enhancement.

5. Creation of Collaborations and Cross-Utilitarian Skills

Dealing with different revenue streams frequently requires an assorted range of abilities. This part investigates how people can foster cross-utilitarian abilities that supplement different undertakings. The formation of cooperative energies between revenue streams upgrades generally speaking adequacy and versatility.

6. Long-Term Manageability and Independence

Various revenue streams add to long haul monetary maintainability. This page digs into how a differentiated pay portfolio upholds monetary freedom, permitting people to support their ideal way of life without overreliance on conventional business.

7. Enhanced Creativity and Innovation

Adjusting different revenue streams encourages innovativeness and development. This part investigates how people took part in different pursuits frequently track down motivation and new thoughts that benefit all parts of their expert and enterprising undertakings.

8. Contributions to Community and Society

Having various revenue streams can stretch out advantages to the local area and society. This page investigates how people with differentiated pay sources might have the ability to add to worthy missions, mentorship projects, or local area advancement drives, making positive effects past private monetary benefits.

Difficulties and Contemplations in Dealing with Numerous Income Streams

While the idea of numerous revenue streams offers critical advantages, it additionally accompanies difficulties and contemplations. This part investigates normal difficulties, for example, using time productively, potential burnout, and the requirement for successful monetary preparation. Systems for defeating these difficulties and it are talked about to upgrade pay enhancement.

1. Effective Time Management

Adjusting different revenue streams demands powerful using time effectively. This page investigates methodologies for focusing on undertakings, defining limits, and upgrading efficiency to guarantee that every revenue stream gets sufficient consideration without prompting burnout.

2. Financial Arranging and Expense Considerations

Dealing with various revenue streams requires cautious monetary preparation. This segment digs into contemplations, for example, planning, charge arranging, and representing the changeability in pay sources. Vital monetary arranging guarantees that pay expansion lines up with by and large monetary objectives.

3. Risk Management and Possibility Planning

Differentiating revenue streams presents extraordinary dangers.

CHAPTER 4: SAVING AND INVESTMENT

Effective Saving Propensities: Building an Establishment for Monetary Security

Developing powerful saving propensities is a foundation of monetary achievement, giving people the instruments to explore vulnerabilities, seek after objectives, and construct a solid future. In this investigation, we dig into the standards and practices that add to a powerful saving outlook, enabling people to gain significant headway on their growing a strong financial foundation venture.

Figuring out the Significance of Saving: An Essential Way to deal with Wealth

Saving is something beyond saving cash; it is an essential way to deal with growing a substantial financial foundation that includes restrained arranging and intentional designation of assets. This part investigates the more extensive meaning of saving, stressing how it fills in as a monetary security net, works with objective accomplishment, and lays the basis for long haul strength.

1. Emergency Asset: Shielding Monetary Well-being

Fabricating and keeping a secret stash is a major saving propensity. This page digs into the significance of having a monetary pad to cover surprising costs, from health related crises to vehicle fixes. A rainy day account gives genuine serenity and safeguards people from the monetary effect of unexpected conditions.

2. Goal-Oriented Saving: Transforming Goals into Reality

Saving considering explicit objectives is a strong inspiration. This segment investigates how people can distinguish and focus on their monetary objectives, whether it's purchasing a home, subsidizing instruction, or making arrangements for retirement. Objective situated saving changes goals into substantial targets, directing people in designating assets successfully.

3. Automated Investment funds: Consistency through Technology

Robotizing investment funds is a pragmatic procedure to guarantee consistency. This page investigates how people can use innovation to set up programmed moves to a bank account. Computerization eliminates the requirement for consistent manual intercession, making saving a consistent and essential piece of one's monetary everyday practice.

4. Pay Yourself First: A Basic Saving Principle

The "pay yourself first" standard is a basic idea in compelling saving. This segment dives into the act of focusing on investment funds prior to distributing assets to different costs. By regarding investment funds as a non-debatable cost, people lay out a proactive way to deal with creating financial momentum.

5. Budgeting for Saving: Adjusting Pay and Expenses

Coordinating saving into an extensive financial plan is fundamental. This page investigates how people can dispense a particular piece of their pay to reserve funds as a feature of their planning cycle. By intentionally overseeing costs and focusing on saving, people make a monetary structure that upholds their drawn out objectives.

6. Frugality and Careful Spending: Amplifying Resources

Rehearsing thriftiness and careful spending adds to compelling saving. This part investigates the significance of evaluating needs versus needs, pursuing deliberate buying choices, and limiting superfluous costs. By taking on a careful way to deal with spending, people boost their assets for saving and establishing financial stability.

7. Regular Monetary Survey: Evaluating Progress

Standard monetary survey are critical for evaluating saving advancement and changing systems depending on the situation. This page investigates the significance of intermittently checking on monetary objectives, following costs, and guaranteeing that saving endeavors line up with developing needs and conditions.

8. Exploring High return Reserve funds Choices: Expanding Returns

Expanding returns on reserve funds includes investigating high return investment funds choices. This part dives into choices, for example, exorbitant premium saving accounts, certificate of deposit (Cds), or other investment vehicles that proposition preferred returns over customary savings accounts. By advancing investment funds methodologies, people improve their growing a substantial financial foundation potential.

9. Debt Reduction as a Saving Procedure: Monetary Liberation

Tending to and paying off past commitments is an essential saving methodology.

This page investigates how people can dispense a part of their assets to obligation reimbursement, opening up future pay for saving and speculation. Obligation decrease lines up with the more extensive objective of accomplishing monetary freedom.

10. Cooperative Saving: Family and Gathering Strategies

Cooperative saving includes pooling assets with relatives, companions, or accomplices to accomplish shared monetary objectives. This part investigates how cooperative saving can intensify assets, upgrade responsibility, and cultivate a feeling of shared monetary obligation. Bunch procedures can be especially powerful for huge scope objectives.

11. Periodic Savings Challenges: Encouraging Motivation

Taking part in Periodic Savings Challenges is a persuasive technique. This page investigates how people can set momentary saving difficulties, whether it's an extended reserve funds run or a particular reserve funds objective inside a set time period. Challenges infuse energy into the saving system and give unmistakable achievements to festivity.

12. Mindset Shift: Review Saving as a Priority

An outlook shift is central to successful saving propensities. This segment dives into the significance of survey saving as fundamentally important instead of an untimely idea. By perceiving the drawn out advantages of saving and embracing a proactive mentality, people set up for supported monetary achievement.

13. Educating Yourself on Monetary Literacy

Monetary education assumes a significant part in successful saving. This page investigates how people can teach themselves on monetary ideas, venture procedures, and growing a strong financial foundation standards. A strong comprehension of individual budget enables people to put forth informed choices and upgrade their saving attempts.

14. Celebrating Reserve funds Achievements: Supporting Success

Commending investment funds achievements builds up sure way of behaving. This segment investigates the significance of recognizing and praising accomplishments along the saving excursion. Whether arriving at a particular reserve funds target or effectively finishing a reserve funds challenge, perceiving achievements propels people to proceed with their restrained saving propensities.

15. Adjusting Saving Methodologies with Life Changes

Life changes frequently require acclimations to saving methodologies. This page investigates how people can adjust their saving propensities because of significant life altering situations, for example, marriage, life as a parent, profession changes, or surprising costs. Adaptability in saving procedures guarantees arrangement with developing conditions.

16. Sustainable Saving Practices: Long haul Commitment

Manageable saving pursues include laying out routines that can be kept up with over the long haul. This part investigates how people can make saving schedules that line up with their way of life and inclinations. Supportable practices add to the improvement of a saving outlook that perseveres all through various life stages.

17. Seeking Proficient Counsel: Monetary Guidance

Looking for proficient counsel can upgrade saving methodologies. This page investigates how people can counsel monetary consultants or organizers to get customized direction on advancing saving, effective money management, and generally speaking monetary preparation. Proficient guidance guarantees that saving endeavors line up with more extensive monetary objectives.

18. Teaching Saving Propensities to Future Generation

Showing saving propensities to people in the future is a generational venture. This part investigates how guardians and coaches can impart saving standards in kids and youthful grown-ups. By cultivating monetary education and capable saving propensities, people add to the monetary prosperity of people in the future.

19. Building Flexibility against Way of life Inflation

Opposing way of life expansion is critical for compelling saving. This page investigates how people can keep away from the impulse to increment spending as pay develops, dispensing extra assets to saving and venture all things being equal. Building versatility against way of life expansion guarantees a practical and restrained saving methodology.

20. Contributing to Retirement Reserve funds: Long haul Security

Adding to retirement reserve funds is an imperative part of successful saving. This segment digs into the significance of focusing on retirement accounts, for example, 401(k) or IRA, to get long haul monetary security. Retirement investment funds add to building a hearty monetary starting point for the later phases of life.

Challenges in Creating Viable Saving Habits

Creating viable saving propensities accompanies its difficulties. This segment investigates normal hindrances, including compulsions to overspend, startling costs, and the requirement for discipline. Systems for defeating these difficulties and it are examined to keep a versatile saving mentality.

1. Temptations to Overspend

The impulse to overspend represents a test to powerful saving. This page investigates procedures for opposing incautious buys, developing careful ways of managing money, and keeping fixed on long haul monetary objectives.

2. Unexpected Costs and Monetary Setbacks

Unforeseen costs and monetary mishaps can upset saving plans. This part dives into the significance of having alternate courses of action, for example, crisis reserves, and changing saving systems in light of unanticipated conditions.

3. Discipline and Consistency

Keeping up with discipline and consistency in saving propensities requires progressing exertion. This page investigates commonsense methods for remaining propelled, laying out schedules, and defeating difficulties connected with keeping a steady saving practice.

4. External Impacts and Friend Pressure

Outer impacts and companion strain can affect saving choices. This part investigates how people can explore cultural assumptions, fight the temptation to contrast what is happening with others, and remain consistent with their saving objectives.

5. Fear of Effective money management and Hazard Aversion

Anxiety toward effective money management and hazard avoidance can obstruct establishing a strong financial foundation. This page investigates procedures for defeating these feelings of trepidation, teaching oneself on speculation standards, and slowly integrating venture systems into a thorough saving arrangement.

6. Procrastination and Postponed Planning

Stalling and postponed arranging present difficulties to powerful saving. This segment investigates how people can beat stalling by putting forth unambiguous objectives, breaking them into sensible advances, and making gradual moves toward building a saving propensity.

7. Balancing Transient Delight and Long haul Goals

Offsetting momentary pleasure with long haul objectives requires cognizant independent direction. This page investigates how people can figure out some kind of harmony between enjoying present joys and focusing on reserve funds for future monetary security.

8. Impact of Monetary Conditions

Monetary circumstances can affect saving procedures. This segment investigates how people can explore monetary variances, change their saving plans in like manner, and influence open doors that emerge during various financial cycles.

9. Impact of Life Transitions

Life advances, like marriage, being a parent, or profession changes, can influence saving propensities. This page investigates how people can proactively change their saving methodologies to line up with new needs and obligations during critical life advances.

10. Overcoming Saving Plateaus

Arriving at saving plateau can deter. This part investigates procedures for defeating levels by rethinking objectives, looking for new difficulties, and integrating inventive saving strategies to reignite inspiration.

Decision: Supporting a Long period of Monetary Wellness

Creating and supporting viable saving propensities is a deep rooted venture that develops with individual conditions, objectives, and goals. This page finishes up the investigation by underlining the getting through effect of developing a saving outlook, exploring difficulties, and adjusting techniques to cultivate a long period of monetary wellbeing.

Investment Choices: Differentiating Your Portfolio

Broadening your venture portfolio includes decisively designating assets across a scope of resources for expand returns while overseeing risk. This investigation dives into different speculation choices, each offering exceptional open doors and contemplations. Understanding these choices engages people to settle on informed choices and construct a strong venture methodology.

1. Stock Market Speculations: Values for Growth

Putting resources into the securities exchange gives an open door to capital appreciation through the acquisition of offers in public corporations. This page investigates the elements of securities exchange speculations, including individual stocks and exchange traded funds (ETFs). While stocks offer likely exceptional yields, they accompany market instability and require an intensive comprehension of the organizations and ventures included.

2. Bonds: Fixed-Income Protections for Stability

Bonds are obligation protections that pay occasional interest and return the head at development. This segment dives into the attributes of securities, including government securities, corporate securities, and civil securities. Securities are viewed as steadier than stocks and can be a significant part of a differentiated portfolio, turning out normal revenue and going about as a fence against market unpredictability.

3. Real Estate Investment: Unmistakable Resources with Pay Potential

Putting resources into land includes buying properties for rental pay or capital appreciation. This page investigates the different types of land ventures, including private and business properties, real estate investment trusts (REITs), and crowdfunding stages. Land offers the potential for both ordinary pay through lease and long haul appreciation.

4. Mutual Assets: Expertly Oversaw Portfolios

Common subsidizes pool cash from various financial backers to put resources into an expanded arrangement of stocks, bonds, or different protections. This part digs into the benefits of common assets, like proficient administration and moment enhancement. Understanding the various kinds of common assets, including file reserves and effectively oversaw reserves, assists financial backers adjust their decisions to their monetary objectives and hazard resilience.

5. Exchange-Traded Fund (ETFs): Adaptable and Cost-Effective

Exchange-Traded Fund (ETFs) are speculation subsidizes exchanged on stock trades, offering a financially savvy method for acquiring openness to different resource classes. This page investigates the advantages of ETFs, like liquidity, enhancement, and lower charges. Understanding how ETFs track explicit lists or areas permits financial backers to fit their portfolios to their venture targets.

6. Cryptocurrency: Digital Assets with High Volatility

Digital money, led by Bitcoin and Ethereum, addresses a moderately new and unstable resource class. This segment investigates the attributes of cryptographic forms of money, including blockchain innovation and decentralized finance (DeFi) applications. While digital money ventures offer expected exceptional yields, they accompany huge instability and require cautious thought of chance resistance.

7. Precious Metals: Fence against Expansion and Financial Uncertainty

Putting resources into valuable metals, like gold and silver, fills in as a fence against expansion and financial vulnerability. This page investigates the job of valuable metals in an enhanced portfolio, featuring their verifiable importance as store-of-significant worth resources. Understanding the elements impacting valuable metal costs assists financial backers with evaluating their possible commitment to a balanced speculation system.

8. Savings Records and Certificate of Deposit (CDs): Security and Liquidity

Conventional bank accounts and Certificate of Deposit (Cds) give an okay choice to protecting capital while procuring revenue. This part investigates the highlights of bank accounts and Compact discs, including liquidity and government store protection. While these choices offer lower returns contrasted with less secure speculations, they give a safe spot to stop assets for transient objectives or crisis investment funds.

9. Options and Subsidiaries: Complex Procedures for Experienced Investors

Choices and subsidiaries are progressed monetary instruments that permit financial backers to support risk or theorize on cost developments. This page dives into the intricacies of choices exchanging, including calls and puts, and the expected purposes of subordinates. These systems require a profound comprehension of market elements and are by and large reasonable for experienced financial backers.

10. Peer-to-Peer Leadng and Crowdfunding: Elective Speculation Platforms

Distributed loaning and crowdfunding stages associate borrowers with individual financial backers. This segment investigates the open doors and dangers related with these elective speculation choices. While they offer the potential for better yields, financial backers ought to painstakingly evaluate the credit hazard and stage unwavering quality prior to taking part in these modern roads.

Risk Management in Investment: Methodologies for Monetary Security

Actually overseeing risk is fundamental for safeguarding capital and accomplishing long haul monetary security. This investigation dives into key standards and methodologies for risk the executives in ventures, engaging people to explore the vulnerabilities of the monetary business sectors while enhancing their establishing a strong financial foundation venture.

1. Diversification: Spreading Chance across Assets

Enhancement includes spreading ventures across various resource classes to lessen openness to any single gamble. This page investigates how a very much expanded portfolio can moderate the effect of market vacillations on in general execution. Vital portion to different ventures, like stocks, bonds, and land, assists financial backers with accomplishing a harmony among chance and return.

2. Asset Designation: Adjusting Speculations to Objectives and Chance Tolerance

Resource assignment is the method involved with circulating speculations among various resource classes in view of a person's monetary objectives, time skyline, and hazard resistance. This part digs into the significance of key resource portion and how it tends to be changed after some time to adjust to evolving conditions. Altering resource distribution guarantees that ventures line up with the financial backer's novel monetary circumstance and goals.

3. Risk Resilience Evaluation: Grasping Individual Speculation Limits

Evaluating risk resilience is a basic move toward developing a venture system. This page investigates the elements impacting risk resistance, including time skyline, monetary objectives, and close to home strength. Understanding one's gamble resilience assists financial backers with settling on educated conclusions about the blend regarding resources in their portfolio and the degree of unpredictability they can easily persevere.

4. Risk-Return Tradeoff: Adjusting Possible Gains and Losses**

The risk return tradeoff is an essential standard in effective financial planning that recognizes the connection between the potential for more significant yields and expanded risk. This segment investigates how financial backers can evaluate their gamble craving and adjust it to their ideal degree of profits. Finding the right equilibrium guarantees that venture choices reflect individual inclinations and monetary targets.

5. Risk Management Instruments: Supporting and Protection Strategies

Risk management instruments, like supporting and protection, give extra layers of security to financial backers. This page investigates how people can utilize choices, fates, and protection items to alleviate explicit dangers in their portfolio. Utilizing these devices requires a complete comprehension of their systems and possible effect on in general gamble openness.

6. Continuous Observing and Rebalancing: Adjusting to Market Changes

Consistent checking and rebalancing include routinely evaluating the exhibition of a venture portfolio and changing distributions on a case by case basis. This segment dives into the significance of remaining informed about economic situations, monetary patterns, and changes in individual speculations. Occasional rebalancing guarantees that the portfolio stays lined up with the financial backer's gamble resilience and monetary objectives.

7. Stress Testing: Assessing Portfolio Resilience

Stress testing includes mimicking different situations to assess how a portfolio would perform under unfavorable circumstances. This page investigates the idea of stress testing and its part in surveying the versatility of a venture technique. Recognizing potential shortcomings permits financial backers to make proactive changes in accordance with improve the general strength of their portfolios.

8. Emergency Planning: Planning for Surprising Monetary Events

Emergency planning includes expecting and planning for surprising monetary occasions that could influence a speculation portfolio. This segment investigates how people can lay out crisis reserves, protection inclusion, and emergency courses of action to explore unexpected conditions. Proactive crisis arranging upgrades monetary strength and safeguards long haul venture goals.

9. Risk-Mindful Speculation Choices: Educated and Smart Choices

Pursuing risk mindful speculation choices implies insightful thought of likely dangers and prizes. This page investigates how financial backers can direct exhaustive examination, survey economic situations, and remain informed about monetary elements affecting their speculations. Fostering a trained way to deal with navigation guarantees that decisions line up with generally speaking gamble the executives systems.

10. Education and Monetary Proficiency: Engaging Informed Choices

Training and monetary proficiency assume an essential part in viable gamble the board. This part dives into how people can constantly teach themselves about venture standards, market elements, and chance variables. Improving monetary education enables financial backers to pursue informed decisions, explore vulnerabilities, and construct a strong speculation technique.

11. Seeking Proficient Guidance: Counselling Monetary Experts

Looking for proficient guidance is an important part of chance administration. This page investigates how people can draw in monetary consultants or organizers to get customized direction on risk evaluation, portfolio development, and generally speaking monetary preparation. Proficient skill gives experiences and methodologies customized to individual conditions.

12. Behavioural Finance: Understanding Psychological Influences

Social money looks at how mental elements impact monetary direction. This part investigates normal social inclinations, like misfortune abhorrence and presumptuousness, and their effect on speculation decisions. Perceiving these predispositions empowers financial backers to go with additional judicious choices and stay away from traps that might emerge from close to home responses to advertise vacillations.

13. Long-Term Point of view: Enduring Transient Volatility

Keeping a drawn out point of view is vital to successful gamble the executives. This page investigates the significance of zeroing in on all-encompassing monetary objectives and fighting the temptation to respond imprudently to momentary market vacillations. A patient and trained approach permits financial backers to climate unpredictability and catch the expected advantages of long haul speculation methodologies.

14. Scenario Planning: Expecting Future Market Conditions

Situation planning includes considering different potential future economic situations and their effect on speculations. This part investigates how financial backers can take part in situation wanting to plan for various monetary situations, loan cost conditions, or international occasions. Expecting potential results upgrades readiness and supports proactive gamble the executives.

15. Regulatory Consistence: Complying to Venture Regulations

Sticking to administrative consistence is vital for overseeing lawful and administrative dangers. This page investigates how financial backers can remain informed about appropriate regulations and guidelines overseeing their speculations. Following lawful prerequisites guarantees that venture choices line up with industry principles and shields against possible legitimate difficulties.

16. Cyber security Measures: Safeguarding Monetary Assets

Network safety measures are fundamental for safeguarding monetary resources in an undeniably advanced scene. This segment dives into the significance of carrying out strong network protection works on, including secure web-based records, encryption, and two-factor verification. Shielding computerized resources upgrades generally risk the board and safeguards against potential digital dangers.

17. Market Exploration and A reasonable level of effort: Informed Choice Making

Directing intensive statistical surveying and an expected level of effort is a basic part of chance administration. This page investigates how financial backers can evaluate the basics of individual speculations, break down market patterns, and remain informed about monetary pointers. Informed dynamic in light of thorough exploration adds to powerful take a chance with relief.

18. Global Financial Patterns: Taking into account Global Factors

Worldwide financial patterns can essentially influence speculation portfolios. This part investigates how people can remain informed about global financial elements, international occasions, and money vacillations. Taking into account worldwide patterns in risk the board methodologies permits financial backers to explore interconnected markets and go with all around informed choices.

19. Environmental, Social, and Governance (ESG) Rules: Feasible Investing

Environmental, Social, and Governance (ESG) models are progressively viewed as in venture choices. This page investigates how ESG variables can be integrated into risk the board systems, adjusting ventures to supportability objectives. Practical money management intends to create positive cultural and natural effects while accomplishing monetary goals.

20. Insurance Systems: Safeguarding Against Explicit Risks

Protection systems supplement by and large gamble the board by giving security against explicit dangers. This segment dives into different protection items, like life coverage, health care coverage, and property protection, and their job in shielding monetary resources. Evaluating protection needs and choosing proper inclusion improves in general gamble versatility.

Lastly; exploring the intricacies of speculation choices and hazard the board requires an insightful and informed approach. This investigation closes by underscoring the significance of nonstop picking up, adjusting techniques to evolving conditions, and keeping a trained obligation to long haul monetary objectives. Building a strong venture technique includes a mix of broadening, risk mindfulness, and a pledge to monetary prosperity.

CHAPTER 5: DEBT MANAGEMENT

Practical Methods for Taking care of and Paying off Debt: A Guide to Monetary Freedom

Paying off debt is a vital stage toward accomplishing monetary soundness and creating financial stability. This investigation gives reasonable tips and techniques to people looking to oversee and diminish their obligation trouble, enabling them to assume command over their monetary excursion.

1. Assessing and Coordinating Debt: Know Your Monetary Landscape

Begin by surveying your debt extensively. List every exceptional debt, including charge cards, advances, and some other monetary commitments. Arrange them in light of financing costs, extraordinary equilibriums, and regularly scheduled installments. Understanding the full extent of your debts is the most vital move toward making a powerful debt decrease plan.

2. Creating a Practical Budget: Laying out Monetary Boundaries

Fostering a sensible spending plan is fundamental for successful Debt Management. Sort your costs, designate explicit sums for necessities, and put away assets for debt reimbursement. This interaction distinguishes regions where spending can be changed and guarantees a make way for meeting both prompt requirements and long haul monetary objectives.

3. Prioritizing Exorbitant Interest rest debt: Handling the Costliest First

Focus on taking care of exorbitant interest debt first. Center around charge cards or advances with the most elevated loan fees, as they contribute fundamentally to in general debt. Apportioning more assets to these obligations speeds up the decrease of revenue installments, permitting you to set aside cash over the long haul.

4. Negotiating Lower Interest Rate: Supporting for Monetary Relief

Contact your banks to arrange lower financing costs. Clear up your monetary circumstance and express your responsibility for reimbursing the debt. Lower loan fees can fundamentally lessen the general expense of obligation and make reimbursement more reasonable.

5. Consolidating Debts: Smoothing out Repayment

Investigate debt combination choices, for example, merging exorbitant premium obligations into a solitary credit with a lower loan cost. This technique smoothes out reimbursement endeavors, improves on your monetary commitments, and may bring about lower regularly scheduled installments.

6. Implementing the debt Snowball Technique: Building Momentum

Consider the debt snowball technique for reimbursement. Begin by taking care of the littlest debts first while making least instalments on bigger debts. As each more modest obligation is cleared, apply the opened up assets to the following debt in line. This technique gathers speed and inspiration as you witness substantial advancement.

7. Utilizing Bonuses and Rewards: Speeding up Repayment

Influence bonuses, for example, charge discounts, work rewards, or startling monetary benefits, to speed up debt reimbursement. Coordinating these assets toward your exceptional obligations can speed up the cycle and add to critical decreases.

8. Generating Extra Income: Enhancing Reimbursement Efforts

Investigate chances to produce extra pay. This could include a side work, independent work, or selling unused things. Enhancing your pay gives additional assets that can be allotted toward obligation reimbursement, hurrying the way to independence from the rat race.

9. Seeking Proficient Exhortation: Counselling Credit Counsellors

Think about looking for proficient exhortation from credit advocates. These experts can give direction on planning, debt management methodologies, and haggling with loan bosses. Their mastery can assist you with exploring testing monetary circumstances and foster an economical arrangement for debt decrease.

10. Avoiding Aggregating New Debt: Breaking the Cycle

As you pursue paying off existing debt, focus on keeping away from the gathering of new debt. Survey your ways of managing money, focus on needs over needs, and practice monetary discipline to forestall falling once again into the pattern of debt.

11. Exploring Debt Settlement: Arranging Decreased Payoffs

Investigate obligation repayment choices, where you haggle with loan bosses to settle obligations for not exactly everything owed. While this approach might influence your credit score, it can give a more sensible goal to those confronting huge monetary difficulty.

12. Understanding Credit Score: Checking and Improvement

Consistently screen your credit score and report. Understanding your credit score assists you with surveying your monetary wellbeing and recognize regions for development. Reliably making on-time installments and paying off past commitments contribute emphatically shockingly score over the long run.

13. Cutting Pointless Expenses: Trim to Save

Distinguish and cut superfluous costs from your spending plan. This could include reevaluating membership administrations, feasting out less often, or tracking down savvy options. Divert the assets saved toward obligation reimbursement to speed up your advancement.

14. Building a Secret stash: Safeguarding against Future Debt

Laying out a secret stash gives a monetary pad to unforeseen costs. Having this asset set up forestalls the need to depend on Mastercards or advances in the midst of monetary strain, safeguarding you from collecting extra obligation.

15. Educating Yourself on Monetary Proficiency: Engaging Informed Decisions

Persistently instruct yourself on monetary education to arrive at informed conclusions about obligation the board and generally speaking monetary preparation. Understanding loan costs, credit terms, and powerful planning outfits you with the information expected to explore the intricacies of individual budget.

16. Staying Inspired: Observing Milestones

Celebrate achievements along your obligation decrease venture. Whether it's taking care of a charge card or arriving at a particular obligation decrease objective, recognizing your advancement keeps you persuaded and supports positive monetary propensities.

17. Building an Emotionally supportive network: Shared Monetary Goals

Share your monetary objectives with a confided in companion, relative, or monetary consultant. Having an emotionally supportive network gives responsibility, consolation, and significant bits of knowledge as you make progress toward obligation decrease and independence from the rat race.

18. Reviewing and Adjusting Your Plan: Adaptability in Monetary Strategies

Consistently survey your obligation decrease plan and make changes depending on the situation. Life conditions might change, and adaptability in your methodology permits you to adjust to new difficulties or open doors for expanded monetary steadiness.

19. Participating in Monetary Conference: Persistent Learning

Take part in monetary classes to extend your insight on obligation the executives, planning, and monetary preparation. Constant learning improves your capacity to go with informed choices and fortifies your monetary astuteness.

20. Long-Term Monetary Preparation: Past Debt Reduction

Incorporate obligation decrease endeavours into a more extensive long haul monetary arrangement. Consider how your obligation decrease techniques line up with objectives, for example, homeownership, retirement arranging, and abundance collection. An all-encompassing methodology guarantees that obligation the board is important for a feasible and extensive monetary future.

In Essence, Dealing with and paying off past commitments is an extraordinary excursion that requires responsibility, vital preparation, and monetary discipline. This investigation finishes up by underscoring the significance of progressing endeavors, constant learning, and a proactive way to deal with accomplishing and supporting independence from the rat race. Carrying out these viable tips positions people to assume command over their monetary prosperity and construct a strong starting point for a prosperous future.

Debt repayment Strategies: Ways to deal with Monetary Freedom

Debt repayment Strategies is a basic part of accomplishing independence from the rat race. This investigation dives into different methodologies people can utilize to really and decisively pay down their obligations, giving a guide to exploring the excursion towards an obligation free future.

1. Snowball Technique: Little Wins for Large Progress

The debt snowball strategy includes taking care of the littlest debts first while making least installments on bigger debts. As every little debts is cleared, the assets recently apportioned to it are diverted to the following littlest debts. This approach makes a feeling of achievement with every obligation wiped out, gathering speed for handling bigger equilibriums.

2. Avalanche Strategy: Focusing on Exorbitant Interest Debts

The debt torrential slide strategy focuses on obligations in light of their financing costs. Begin by taking care of the obligation with the most noteworthy loan fee, then, at that point, logically tackle debt with lower rates. This approach limits the general interest paid, possibly speeding up the obligation reimbursement process.

3. Debt Consolidation: Smoothing out Repayment

Debt Consolidation includes consolidating various debts into a solitary advance or credit account. This can improve on reimbursement by furnishing a solitary regularly scheduled installment with a possibly lower loan fee. In any case, it's urgent to painstakingly evaluate terms and charges related with combination to guarantee it lines up with your monetary objectives.

4. Debt Management Plan (DMP): Proficient Assistance

A DMP is an organized reimbursement plan worked with by credit guiding organizations. Leasers might consent to bring down loan costs and defer expenses to help the arrangement. Working with a credit directing office can furnish master direction in haggling with banks and laying out a practical reimbursement plan.

5. Balance Move: Gaining by Low-Interest Offers

Consider moving exorbitant premium Visa offsets to a card with a lower financing cost, frequently through a limited time balance move offer. This technique can assist with lessening interest installments and speed up obligation reimbursement. Be aware of move charges and the length of the special rate.

6. Bi-Weekly Payment: Speeding up Reimbursement Momentum

Making every other week installments rather than regularly scheduled installments can bring about an additional installment every year. This approach exploits the schedule's construction, really giving an extra yearly commitment toward debt decrease and possibly diminishing the general reimbursement period.

7. Debt Repayment: Arranging Diminished Payoffs

Debt repayment includes haggling with leasers to settle an obligation for not exactly everything owed. While this approach might affect credit score, it can offer alleviation for people confronting huge monetary difficulty. Proficient help might be valuable in exploring the exchange cycle.

8. Zero-Aggregate Planning: Dispensing Each Dollar

Lose planning requires dispensing each dollar of pay to explicit classifications, ruling out unallocated spending. This trained methodology guarantees that all suitable assets are coordinated toward obligation reimbursement, cultivating a proactive and deliberate position toward monetary objectives.

9. Side Hustles and Bonuses: Supporting Reimbursement Capacity

Investigate side hustles or exploit unforeseen bonuses, for example, rewards or expense discounts, to speed up debt reimbursement. Enhancing ordinary income with extra supports upgrades your ability to rapidly settle debts more.

10. Automated Payments: Guaranteeing Consistency

Set up automated payment for your debts to guarantee consistency and stay away from missed cutoff times. Mechanization lessens the gamble of late installments, charges, and expected harm amazingly score. It likewise imparts discipline in your monetary daily practice.

11. Peer Backing: Responsibility and Encouragement

Take part in peer support gatherings or discussions where people share their obligation reimbursement ventures. The feeling of responsibility and consolation from others confronting comparable difficulties can give inspiration and significant bits of knowledge.

12. Financial Bonuses: Key Allocation

While getting monetary bonuses, like a legacy or lottery rewards, decisively distribute a piece to obligation reimbursement. While it very well may be enticing to enjoy different regions, focusing on obligation decrease contributes essentially to your drawn out monetary prosperity.

13. Credit Counselling: Proficient Guidance

Credit counselling administrations give proficient direction on obligation the board, planning, and monetary preparation. These administrations can assist people with fostering an organized arrangement for reimbursing obligations, haggle with banks, and gain significant monetary schooling.

14. Emergency Asset: Protecting Against Future Debt

Keeping a secret stash goes about as a monetary security net, forestalling the need to depend on Visas or credits for startling costs. Having this asset set up shields against gathering new obligation during unexpected conditions.

15. Gradual Way of life Changes: Supportable Debt Reduction

Think about making progressive way of life changes in accordance with let loose assets for debt reimbursement. This could include cutting pointless costs, rethinking bills, or tracking down additional savvy options. Manageable changes add to continuous obligation decrease endeavors.

16. Debt Reimbursement Difficulties: Confronting Mishaps with Resilience

Recognize that debt reimbursement might include difficulties. Surprising costs, changes in pay, or different misfortunes can happen. Foster flexibility by expecting difficulties and having alternate courses of action set up to keep focused notwithstanding hindrances.

17. Celebrate Achievements: Building up Sure Behaviour

Celebrate achievements along your obligation reimbursement venture. Whether taking care of a Mastercard, arriving at a particular debt decrease objective, or accomplishing obligation free status in a specific classification, recognizing achievements supports positive monetary way of behaving.

18. Debt Reimbursement Applications and Apparatuses: Improving Organization

Investigate debt reimbursement applications and apparatuses to improve association and following. These instruments can assist you with picturing progress, put forth objectives, and remain inspired. From planning applications to obligation result number crunchers, utilizing innovation can smooth out your obligation reimbursement methodology.

19. Credit Score Checking: Following Improvement

Routinely screen your credit score as you reimburse obligations. Seeing upgrades in your credit score fills in as uplifting feedback and highlights the substantial headway you're making toward independence from the rat race.

20. Financial Instruction: Engaging Informed Choices

Consistently instruct yourself on monetary proficiency and debt the board systems. Understanding loan fees, reimbursement choices, and individual budget standards enables you to pursue educated decisions and explore the intricacies regarding debt reduction actually.

Setting out on an excursion to reimburse debt requires a mix of vital preparation, discipline, and flexibility. This investigation closes by stressing the significance of picking an obligation reimbursement system that lines up with your exceptional monetary circumstance and objectives. By executing these different procedures, people can explore the way to independence from the rat race with certainty and versatility.

CHAPTER 6: ASSET BUILDING

Building and Diversifying Asset: An Outline for Monetary Growth

Building and Diversifying Asset are fundamental stages in making long haul monetary progress. This investigation gives a complete aide on techniques to construct and broaden resources, engaging people to develop a strong and versatile monetary portfolio.

1. Emergency Asset: An Establishment for Monetary Security

Begin by laying out a rainy day account to cover three to a half year of everyday costs. This asset goes about as a monetary wellbeing net, giving steadiness during surprising conditions and forestalling the need to exchange interests in crises.

2. Savings Records and Certificate of Deposit (Cds): Generally safe Foundations

Use conventional bank accounts and Cds for generally safe groundworks in building resources. While these choices might offer lower returns, they give liquidity and steadiness, making them appropriate for momentary monetary objectives and safeguarding capital.

3. Stock Market Ventures: Values for Long haul Growth

Think about putting resources into the securities exchange for long haul development potential. Values, including individual stocks and exchanged traded fund (ETFs), offer the chance for capital value increase over the long haul. Research and enhance ventures to relieve risk and line up with your monetary goals.

4. Real Estate Investment: Substantial Resources with Income Potential

Investigate land speculations for the purpose of broadening resources. Private or business properties, real estate investment trusts (REITs), and crowdfunding stages give roads to pay age and long haul appreciation. Broadening across land classes improves portfolio strength.

5. Bonds: Fixed-Pay Protections for Stability

Integrate securities into your portfolio for soundness and normal pay. Government bonds, corporate bonds, and corporate bonds offer fixed revenue installments, filling in as an offset to more unpredictable value ventures. Expanding bond property across various backers and spans adds further dependability.

6. Mutual Assets: Expertly Oversaw Portfolios

Think about shared assets for a broadened, expertly oversaw portfolio. These assets pool cash from different financial backers to put resources into a blend of stocks, bonds, or different protections. Pick reserves lined up with your gamble resistance and monetary objectives to accomplish wide market openness.

7. Exchange-Traded Fund (ETFs): Adaptable and Cost-Effective

Enhance with ETFs, which are like common assets yet exchange on stock trades. ETFs offer adaptability, liquidity, and ordinarily lower expenses. They track different lists, areas, or wares, permitting financial backers to broaden across a large number of resources.

8. Precious Metals: Fence against Financial Uncertainty

Incorporate valuable metals, like gold and silver, in your resource portfolio as a fence against financial vulnerability. Valuable metals generally hold esteem during monetary slumps, giving a store of riches. Consider expanding a piece of your portfolio with these substantial resources.

9. Cryptocurrency: Arising Advanced Assets

Investigate the capability of digital money as a component of an enhanced portfolio. Computerized resources like Bitcoin and Ethereum offer open doors for development however accompany higher instability. Research and comprehend the dangers prior to designating a part of your resources for this arising resource class.

10. Retirement Accounts: Long haul Wealth Accumulation

Amplify commitments to retirement accounts, for example, 401(k)s and IRAs, for long haul abundance collection. Exploit boss matching commitments and assessment benefits to support your retirement investment funds. Broaden inside these records to line up with your gamble resistance and time skyline.

11. Health Savings Accounts (HSAs): Triple Assessment Benefits

Use HSAs for triple tax reductions. Commitments are charge deductible, income develop tax-exempt, and withdrawals for qualified clinical costs are tax-exempt. HSAs can act as a significant device for building resources while tending to medical services costs.

12. Education Savings Accounts: Putting resources into Future Generations

Distribute assets to schooling bank accounts, like 529 plans, to put resources into the future training of yourself, your youngsters, or other relatives. These duty advantaged accounts work with long haul anticipating instructive costs.

13. Business Possession: Innovative Ventures

Consider pioneering adventures or business proprietorship as a method for building resources. Claiming a business can give potential to huge returns, yet it requires cautious preparation, the executives, and chance evaluation. Expand by putting resources into various business areas.

14. Art and Collectibles: Unmistakable Investments

Enhance with unmistakable speculations like craftsmanship and collectibles. While these resources might require specific information, they can add to portfolio enhancement. Be aware of stockpiling, protection, and market patterns while thinking about these contemporary ventures.

15. Investment Properties: Rental Income and Appreciation

Put resources into land properties for rental pay and likely appreciation. This procedure gives a double advantage of ordinary pay and long haul development. Select properties in essential areas and direct careful statistical surveying for informed venture choices.

16. Dividend Stocks: Pay Producing Equities

Incorporate profit paying stocks in your portfolio to produce recurring, automated revenue. Profit stocks give customary money payouts, adding to by and large portfolio pay. Select stocks with a background marked by steady profits and potential for capital appreciation.

17. Annuities: Reliable Revenue Streams

Investigate annuities for ensured revenue streams in retirement. While intricate, specific kinds of annuities can turn out a consistent revenue, offering a degree of monetary security. Grasp the terms, expenses, and suggestions prior to integrating annuities into your resource portfolio.

Fabricating and expanding resources require a dynamic and vital methodology. This investigation closes by underlining the significance of constant observing, transformation, and expansion to encourage a versatile monetary portfolio. By carrying out these procedures, people can develop a strong resource base that lines up with their objectives and endures the intricacies of the monetary scene.

Real Estate Investment: Creating Wealth through Property

1. Residential Real Estate: Homeownership and Rental Income

- Investigate open doors in private land, whether through homeownership or buying properties for rental pay.

- Consider market patterns, area, and potential for property appreciation while choosing private land speculations.

2. Commercial Real Estate: Enhancing with Pay Producing Properties

- Differentiate your land portfolio with business properties like places of business, retail spaces, or modern units.

- Business land can turn out reliable rental revenue and potential for appreciation, with various gamble factors than private properties.

3. Real Estate Investment Trusts (REITs): Uninvolved Interest in Genuine Estate

- Put resources into REITs, which are public corporations that own, work, or money pay creating land.

- REITs give a detached method for getting to housing markets and frequently offer appealing profits to financial backers.

4. Real Estate Crowdfunding: Taking part in Aggregate Investments

- Investigate land crowdfunding stages to partake in aggregate ventures with moderately lower capital prerequisites.

- These stages permit you to put resources into explicit land projects close by different financial backers, giving enhancement.

Stock Market Investment Opportunity: Exploring Values for Growth

5. Blue-Chip Stocks: Stable Speculations with Profit Potential

- Think about putting resources into blue-chip loads of deeply grounded, monetarily sound organizations.

- Blue-chip stocks frequently give security, potential for capital appreciation, and may offer profits to investors.

6. Technology Stocks: Profiting by Advancement and Growth

 - Investigate amazing open doors in innovation stocks, which can offer high development potential driven by advancement.

 - Tech organizations at the front line of industry patterns might give open doors to significant returns.

7. Dividend Stocks: Creating Uninvolved Income

 - Put resources into profit paying stocks to create recurring, automated revenue through normal profit payouts.

 - Organizations with a background marked by reliable profit installments can add to a consistent revenue source.

8. Emerging Markets: Taking advantage of Development Opportunities

- Expand your stock portfolio by investigating amazing open doors in developing business sectors.

- Developing business sector stocks can furnish openness to economies with high development potential, however they additionally accompany higher unpredictability.

Other Investment Opportunity: Investigating Assorted Avenues

9. Cryptocurrency: Computerized Resources with High Possible Returns

- Investigate the universe of digital currency, like Bitcoin and Ethereum, for possible significant yields.

- Digital currencies offer a decentralized and creative speculation choice, yet they accompany critical instability.

10. Precious Metals: Supporting Against Monetary Uncertainty

- Consider putting resources into valuable metals like gold and silver as a fence against financial vulnerability.

- Valuable metals have generally filled in as a store of significant worth and can be an enhancement device in a speculation portfolio.

11. Exchange-Traded Funds (ETFs): Enhanced Portfolios in a Solitary Investment

- Put resources into ETFs for an enhanced portfolio that tracks a particular record, area, or resource class.

- ETFs give an effective method for enhancing without purchasing individual protections.

12. Peer-to-peer Leading: Taking part in Elective Loaning Platforms

- Investigate shared loaning stages to take part in elective loaning open doors.

- By loaning straightforwardly to people or independent companies, you might possibly acquire better yields contrasted with customary investment accounts.

13. Sustainable Speculations: Lining up with ESG Principles

- Consider economical ventures that line up with ESG standards, zeroing in on natural, social, and administration factors.

- ESG contributing permits you to help organizations with dependable strategic policies while possibly accomplishing monetary returns.

Key Ways to deal with Investment Opportunities

14. Dollar-Cost Averaging: Steady Money management Over Time

- Execute a minimizing risk system by reliably contributing a decent sum at customary stretches.

- This approach decreases the effect of market unpredictability and permits you to aggregate more offers when costs are lower.

15. Long-Term Investment Skyline: Exploiting Compound Growth

- Take on a drawn out speculation skyline to profit by the force of compound development.

- Contributing with an emphasis on the long haul permits your resources for develop dramatically over the long haul.

16. Risk management: Broadening and Resource Allocation

- Alleviate risk through broadening and vital resource distribution.

- Broadening across various resource classes, like land, stocks, and different ventures, helps spread chance and upgrade in general portfolio flexibility.

17. Continuous learning: Remaining Informed and Adjusting Strategies

- Remain informed about market patterns, financial turns of events, and speculation amazing open doors.

- Persistent learning empowers you to adjust your venture methodologies in view of changing circumstances and jump all over new chances.

18. Consulting Monetary Consultants: Proficient Guidance

- Look for direction from monetary guides to foster a customized speculation system.

- Monetary counselors can give bits of knowledge, direct gamble appraisals, and assist with adjusting your ventures to your monetary objectives.

Creating financial wellbeing through land, stocks, and different speculation valuable open doors requires an insightful and broadened approach. This investigation closes by stressing the significance of vital preparation, risk the executives, and ceaseless learning in making a different and strong speculation portfolio. By investigating these valuable open doors with tirelessness and adjusting to changing economic situations, people can explore the intricacies of the investment landscape and work towards long-term financial success.

CHAPTER 7: WEALTH PRESERVATION

Systems for Saving and Safeguarding Wealth Shielding Monetary Success

1. Estate Planning: Organizing for Generational Wealth

- Participate in far reaching domain wanting to guarantee a smooth exchange of abundance to people in the future.

- Use instruments like wills, trusts, and legal authorities to frame your desires and limit charge suggestions.

2. Asset Protection Trusts: Protecting Abundance from Creditors

- Consider laying out resource assurance trusts to safeguard resources from likely lenders.

- These trusts give a degree of insurance against lawful cases, safeguarding abundance for expected recipients.

3. Diversification: Spreading Risk Across Asset Classes

- Keep an expanded speculation portfolio to spread risk across various resource classes.

- Expansion safeguards against misfortunes in any single speculation and improves generally portfolio strength.

4. Insurance Coverage: Relieving Risks and Liabilities

- Audit and update protection inclusion routinely to relieve dangers and liabilities.

- Sufficient inclusion for wellbeing, life, property, and obligation protection safeguards gathered abundance from unexpected occasions.

5. Tax Planning: Advancing Systems for Expense Efficiency

- Execute charge proficient techniques to limit the effect on amassed abundance.

- Work with charge experts to investigate tax breaks, allowances, and speculation structures that line up with your monetary objectives.

6. Legal Structures: Picking Ideal Business Entities

- Select ideal lawful structures for business substances to limit legitimate and monetary dangers.

- Limited Liability Companies (LLCs) give a degree of detachment among individual and business resources.

7. Regular Monetary Audits: Checking and Changing Strategies

- Direct ordinary monetary surveys to screen the presentation of ventures and change systems on a case by case basis.

- Remain proactive in adjusting to changing economic situations and life conditions.

8. Trusts for Minor Recipients: Guaranteeing Capable Abundance Transfer

- Lay out trusts for minor recipients to guarantee capable abundance move.

- Trusts can direct the way that resources are overseen and appropriated, giving direction and assurance to more youthful relatives.

9. Pre-Nuptial and Post-Nuptial Arrangements: Explaining Monetary Expectations

- Consider pre-matrimonial or present marital settlements on explain monetary assumptions and safeguard individual resources.

- These arrangements give a lawful system to resource division in case of a separation.

10. Risk Management Systems: Recognizing and Moderating Risks

- Execute risk management techniques to distinguish and relieve likely dangers to collected riches.

- This incorporates evaluating market gambles, monetary patterns, and outside factors that might influence monetary steadiness.

11. Charitable Giving: Generosity as an Abundance Safeguarding Tool

- Participate in key magnanimous giving for the purpose of abundance protection.

- Laying out altruistic establishments or adding to causes lines up with humanitarian objectives while possibly giving tax reductions.

12. Privacy Measures: Shielding Individual and Monetary Information

- Go to protection lengths to defend individual and monetary data.

- Safeguard against fraud and extortion by carrying out secure practices for online records, reports, and exchanges.

13. Family Administration: Laying out Clear Family Protocols

- Lay out family administration designs to frame clear conventions for abundance the board.

- Open correspondence and characterized jobs assist with guaranteeing family solidarity and monetary congruity across ages.

14. Long-Term Care Planning: Tending to Medical services Expenses

- Plan for long haul care necessities to address potential medical services costs.

- Long haul care protection and different techniques can assist with safeguarding collected abundance from the monetary effect of clinical consideration.

15. Emergency Funds: Getting ready for Unexpected Monetary Events

- Keep up with crisis assets to cover unexpected monetary occasions without draining venture portfolios.

- Having fluid resources promptly accessible gives a monetary wellbeing net.

16. Continued Orientation: Remaining Informed About Monetary Strategies

- Constantly teach yourself about developing monetary methodologies and abundance protection procedures.

- Remaining informed engages you to adjust to changing financial circumstances and arising open doors.

17. Crisis Readiness: Creating Possibility Plans

- Foster alternate courses of action for monetary emergencies, financial slumps, or unanticipated occasions.

- Having a thoroughly examined plan limits the effect of emergencies on gathered riches.

18. Regular Lawful Check-Ups: Guaranteeing Authoritative Document are up to Date

- Lead normal lawful check-ups to guarantee that wills, trusts, and other authoritative records are state-of-the-art.

- Changes in private conditions or regulations might require updates to legitimate designs.

Safeguarding and safeguarding wealth requires a comprehensive and proactive methodology. This investigation closes by underlining the significance of coordinating different systems, remaining informed, and adjusting to evolving conditions. By carrying out these abundance conservation measures, people can shield their monetary achievement and guarantee the drawn out supportability of amassed abundance across ages.

Estate planning and risk mitigation: Getting Monetary Legacies

1. Comprehensive Will and Testament: Organizing Your Intentions

- Foster a complete will that plainly frames your goals for the conveyance of resources.

- Indicate recipients, assign gatekeepers for minor youngsters, and address explicit inheritances to guarantee your desires are completed.

2. Revocable Living Trust: Trying not to Probate and Guarantee Privacy

- Consider laying out a revocable living trust to stay away from probate and keep up with security.

- Resources set in a living trust can pass straightforwardly to recipients without the requirement for court contribution, speeding up the exchange cycle.

3. Power of Attorney: Delegating Confided in Choice Makers

  - Assign a full legal authority for monetary and medical services choices.

  - Selecting confided in people to settle on choices for your benefit in case of inadequacy guarantees a consistent progress and mitigates monetary dangers.

4. Healthcare Intermediary: Guaranteeing Clinical Choice Continuity

  - Name a medical care intermediary to settle on clinical choices as per your inclinations.

  - This guarantees that your medical care wishes are regarded and that choices line up with your qualities and convictions.

5. Guardianship Assignment: Accommodating Minor Children

- Obviously assign watchmen for minor youngsters in your home arrangement.

- This basic step guarantees that your kids are really focused on by people you confide in case of your insufficiency or passing.

6. Life Protection: Giving Monetary Security to Beneficiaries

- Use disaster protection to give monetary security to your recipients.

- Disaster protection continues can assist with covering obligations, memorial service expenses, and offer continuous help for wards.

7. Trusts for Resource Security: Defending Against Creditors

- Carry out trusts for resource assurance to defend abundance against possible banks.

- Unavoidable trusts, like prodigal trusts, can protect resources and accommodate the requirements of recipients while limiting openness to lawful cases.

8. Business Progression Planning: Guaranteeing Smooth Transitions

- Foster a business progression plan in the event that you own a business.

- Obviously frame the progress of proprietorship and the board to alleviate disturbances and safeguard the worth of the business.

Home preparation, combined with risk relief techniques, frames an establishment for building a versatile monetary inheritance. This investigation highlights the significance of an all-encompassing methodology, nonstop surveys, and expert joint effort to explore intricacies and shield your abundance for people in the future. By executing these systems, people can guarantee the protection of their monetary inheritances while limiting dangers and amplifying the advantages of insightful preparation.

THE END